MW00709786

IMAGES
*of America*

# WNAX 570 RADIO
## 1922–2007

This map shows the coverage area of WNAX. It can be heard beyond the regions shown, depending on weather conditions. In October 1973, Jay Nebben, attached to Fighter Squadron 92, was returning to the United States from duty in Southeast Asia. About 800 miles west of Hawaii, he picked up WNAX on his radio while on the deck of the aircraft carrier. The signal faded after about five minutes. In 1990, he wrote to the station to tell of the incident.

*On the cover:* The transmitter building of radio station WNAX, near Mission Hill, South Dakota, is the symbol of a powerful broadcasting company which influenced the history of Yankton, South Dakota, and the lives of people in its five-state listening area.

IMAGES

*of America*

# WNAX 570 RADIO
## 1922–2007

Marilyn Kratz and Stan Ray

ARCADIA

Copyright © 2006 Marilyn Kratz and Stan Ray
ISBN 0-7385-4019-6

Published by Arcadia Publishing
Charleston SC, Chicago IL, Portsmouth NH, San Francisco CA

Printed in the United States of America

Library of Congress Catalog Card Number: 2005937812

For all general information contact Arcadia Publishing at:
Telephone 843-853-2070
Fax 843-853-0044
E-mail sales@arcadiapublishing.com
For customer service and orders:
Toll-Free 1-888-313-2665

Visit us on the Internet at http://www.arcadiapublishing.com

This book is dedicated to the station managers, entertainers, radio
engineers, and other staff members who made WNAX a powerful
voice in the Northern Plains, to the memory of Debra Kohn, and to our
spouses for their patience and encouragement.

–Marilyn Kratz and Stan Ray

# CONTENTS

# ACKNOWLEDGMENTS

We are grateful to the following people who provided photographs and information needed to make this book as accurate as possible: Don and Dolores Benson, Gene Brinkmeyer, Les and Pete Ehresmann, Gene Fiscus, Don Fuerst, Hazel German, Dave Geisler Sr. and Jr., Kathy Grow, Jane Gurney, Chris Hilson, Clinton Kaser, Robert Karolevitz, Jill Karolevitz, Marie Killian, Albert Klasi, Betty Knau, Ernest Kratz, Don Kruml, Lou Ella Machin, Ed Miedema, Jean Lange Neiden, Judy O'Connell, Betty and Larry and Mary Ann O'Malley, Judith Tincher Peterson, Judy Ray, Don Rasmussen, Doug Ray, Lloyd Reedstrom, Doug Sall, Harry and Wynn Speece, Tom Steinbach, Nathan (Bob) Steinbach, Linda Stephenson, Clifton and Dennis Todd, Lois Varvel, Choyce Vilhauer, Woody Vollmer, Howard Willson, *Yankton Daily Press and Dakotan*, the current staff at WNAX, and Evelyn Zimmerman. We also wish to thank our editor Ann Marie Lonsdale for her assistance and support. We apologize if we have omitted the names of any of the many people who helped with the book.

# INTRODUCTION

June, 1939—my first days at a radio station I was to work with for the next 66 years, and grateful for every one of those years. I had just graduated from Drake University and was eager to work in radio. I began by reading the "funnies" on the air with Art Smith at the Cowles Radio Station in Des Moines, Iowa. He recommended me for the job of continuity writer at the newest Cowles acquisition radio station WNAX in Yankton, South Dakota. How lucky I was to become part of this station, so eager to serve well in every way—farm, home, business, daily living—the people in a five-state area of North and South Dakota, Iowa, Minnesota, and Nebraska.

I soon became Women's Director at WNAX. I began a lifelong career in 1941 as Your Neighbor Lady, serving the everyday living needs of the women of the area just as the station had long been serving the men by highlighting farming needs. I traveled throughout the station's coverage area, broadcasting live, meeting women, establishing a special contact—a special relationship—which grew and grew and is still strong and gratifying all these years later.

The station also met my needs in every way it could. My daily radio program had progressed nicely for four years. Then I married in 1945, and when my first baby was on the way, I went to Bob Tincher, station manager at the time, to tell him I would have to leave WNAX when the baby was born. He thought for a moment, then said, "No, we'll just move the microphone into your home." His wise response pleased me and allowed me to create a special new approach to women's broadcasting which became a mainstay to the large midwestern home-geared audience. It was as if my listeners were there with me, visiting, learning together, helping each other. And my mail grew and grew, making my listeners a vital part of our working together. It required eight women to open the thousands of letters I received and fill orders for my sponsors. My listeners and I got to know each other in a personal way.

That attitude, that approach to serving this great midwestern area, carried on through the developing years of WNAX and has been evident in all areas of its broadcasting ever since. The managers of the station knew what the five state area needed in the way of information, entertainment, and help in developing a strong, intelligent living and working area. There is still personal contact with listeners.

WNAX has been fortunate in finding good people to staff the station from top management right on down through every area, all of whom take seriously their commitment to serve the listeners. Like me, they have found the work satisfying and gratifying. It has always been a great place to work. We who have worked at WNAX over the years are grateful to this station and proud to be a part of such a giving business. We will always maintain its quality and contribution to the area.

—Wynn Speece

Shown here is Wynn Speece, Your Neighbor Lady.

# One

# THE GURNEY YEARS

In May 1922, E. C. "Al" Madson helped establish Dakota Radio Apparatus Company in Yankton, South Dakota. He and Chan Gurney started experimenting with radio transmitting. They set up a simple broadcasting station on the second floor over a restaurant on Walnut Street near Third Street using plans in a Popular Mechanics magazine. They used a "morning glory horn" from an Edison phonograph for their microphone and placed a radio receiver in the restaurant. To test their microphone, they ordered sandwiches and coffee. When the restaurant owner delivered their order a few minutes later, they knew their set worked. Madson applied for a license to operate a sending station. It was granted on November 9, 1922. The assigned call letters were WNAX: W indicated a newly-licensed station, N for North, A for American, and X for "experimental." On November 25, 1922, the station broadcast music as part of the 50th anniversary of First National Bank (now First Dakota National Bank) in Yankton. Concerts featuring local musicians followed. With no advertisement to support the station, it broadcast intermittently. Reception was often marred with static. In 1923, Madson, shown here in the first transmitter studio, packed their broadcasting equipment away in a flour barrel until 1925 when they gave it another try.

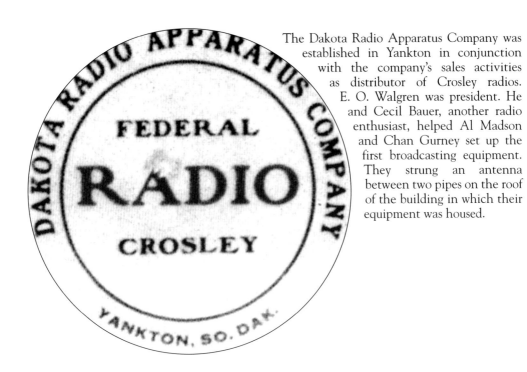

The Dakota Radio Apparatus Company was established in Yankton in conjunction with the company's sales activities as distributor of Crosley radios. E. O. Walgren was president. He and Cecil Bauer, another radio enthusiast, helped Al Madson and Chan Gurney set up the first broadcasting equipment. They strung an antenna between two pipes on the roof of the building in which their equipment was housed.

John Chandler "Chan" Gurney was the son of Deloss Butler "D. B." Gurney, president of Gurney Seed and Nursery company. In 1938, Chan was elected to the U.S. Senate, serving two terms. He was then appointed to the Civil Aeronautics Board by President Truman. In the years before the Gurney family bought WNAX, Al Madson was president and chief engineer for the struggling broadcasting company. Chan Gurney was the announcer.

D. B. Gurney, whose seed and nursery business became one of the largest in the country, discovered his main competitor was achieving great success through the use of radio advertising. Chan investigated the situation and recommended his father buy WNAX to advertise his business. D. B. Gurney bought the station for $2,000. On February 28, 1927, listeners heard, for the first time, "This is station WNAX, House of Gurney in Yankton."

The Gurneys moved the station from the Winter Garden, an entertainment spot in the basement of Brecht Drugstore on Yankton's main street where it had been set up in 1926, to this house at 503 Pine Street, the home of D. B. Gurney. Broadcasts originated in a front room while studios were prepared in the Gurney building. Heavy drapings of monk's cloth on the walls muted outside sounds and echoes. Visitors sat in the living and dining rooms to watch broadcasts.

The first announcers for WNAX after Gurneys bought the station included, from left to right, Bill Goodrich, Earl Williams (seated), Joe Salvatori, and Chan Gurney. They are shown in the broadcast room set up in the front parlor of the Gurney home. Electric fans kept the equipment from overheating. The transformer was submerged in transmission oil in Henrietta Gurney's lard crock to keep it cool. Henrietta made sure the studio was spotlessly clean.

D. B. Gurney's brother Phil, seed sales manager for the nursery, announced the entertainers, which included students from Yankton College and musicians from the community. The station became an immediate success after Gurneys bought it. It received 8,452 telegrams in response to an Old Fiddlers' Contest in March 1927, prompting the Gurneys to set up a Western Union receiving station in their building. A person in Texas was the winner in a contest to find their most distant listener in 1927.

Ed Gurney, D. B.'s brother, was known as "Our Radio Philosopher." Every Sunday evening, for one hour, he gave advice on subjects aimed to make young men become upstanding and successful citizens. D. B. Gurney's brothers George, Philip, and Ed joined the staff as on-air salesmen for the many Gurney products.

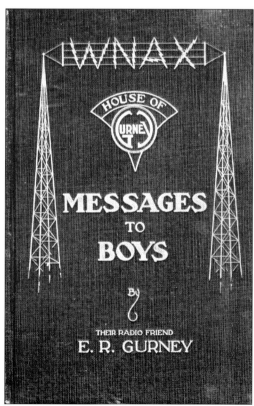

In 1929, Ed Gurney's talks for young boys on WNAX were published in this book and offered for sale by the station. It was printed on cornstalk paper.

Syd Gurney, son of George Gurney, D. B. Gurney's brother, was the garden expert for the station. He answered questions sent in by listeners to his program. He published the nursery company's seed catalog for many years.

Frank Hobbs and Violet Nelson shared their songs with the WNAX listening audience in the late 1920s. They were members of two musical families in Yankton. Violet was the first paid entertainer at WNAX. In the months when the broadcasts originated from the Gurney home, the windows in the front parlor, which extended to the floor, were opened so music could waft out onto the porch where people gathered to dance.

The Royal Serenaders Band won the "Battle of the Bands" contest at WNAX radio in 1927. Members were, from left to right, Clayton Dostal, trombone; Ed Rehurek, trumpet; Dewey Drappeau, sousaphone; Tom Ptak, drums and vocals; Steve Ptak, fiddle, banjo, and vocals; Adeline Wagner, piano; John Dostal, saxophone; Johnny Matuska, clarinet, and Ray Kuca, saxophone. Tom Ptak was the director.

Gurney's Concert Orchestra is shown in the 1930s. This was just one of many small groups and soloists who entertained live over radio station WNAX for many years in its early broadcast history. In 1928, the Gurney Orchestra was awarded a trophy as "the Most Popular Radio Orchestra" in a national publication called Radio Digest.

WNAX entertainers were expected to do their part to advertise Gurney products. Here are Jada Wyman (left) and Bill Goodrich, who became known as the "Battery Boys," to sell WNAX car batteries. Both men played with other musical groups also.

Jack O'Malley came to Yankton in 1927 to participate in a fiddling contest and stayed to become one of the station's most popular entertainers. He performed his unique blend of singing and fiddling, playing strictly by ear, for 35 years on WNAX. Chan Gurney nicknamed him Happy Jack because "he could not only fiddle with the best of them, but he was happy all the time." He is pictured on the left, receiving congratulations from George Gurney after 20 years with the station.

This was part of the WNAX staff in 1928. From left to right, they are (first row) C. Earl Williams, Happy Jack O'Malley, Alice Williams, M. Salvatori, C. Horst, E. Gross, and Jada Wyman; (second row) F. Hobbs, J. Fejfar, Zeke Stout, C. Marquardt, Paul Meilenberg, Ruth Curry, Isabel Gennrich, and J. Walsh Jr.; (third row) Violet Nelson, Don Sigloh, Joe Salvatori, Chandler Gurney, Arthur Harring, Albin Seliskar, D. Christensen, and M. Burns.

Lawrence Welk and his Novelty Band left North Dakota in the winter of 1927 on their way to New Orleans. By the time they got to Yankton, they were too cold and tired to continue. Chan Gurney offered them a one-week contract with WNAX, which they accepted gratefully. From left to right, they are Paul Donnelley, Gordon Mailey, "Spider" Webb, Jim Garvey, Lawrence Welk, and Rolley Chesney.

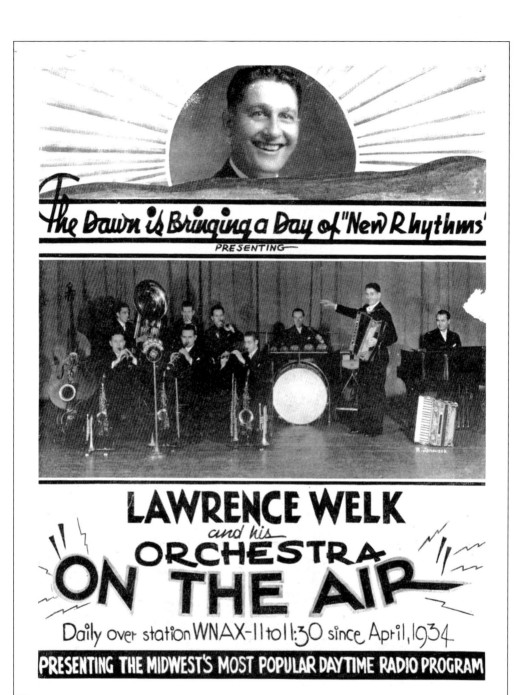

The Dawn is Bringing a Day of "New Rhythms"

PRESENTING—

LAWRENCE WELK
and his
ORCHESTRA
ON THE AIR

Daily over station WNAX-11 to 11:30 since April, 1934

PRESENTING THE MIDWEST'S MOST POPULAR DAYTIME RADIO PROGRAM

During their almost 10 years on WNAX, Lawrence Welk changed his band's name from the Lawrence Welk Novelty Band to the Hotsy Totsy Boys, and later the Honolulu Fruit Gum Band.

Featuring America's Foremost Dance *presents New Rhythms*

ACCORDIONIST

Known from
Coast to Coast
Through
the Presentations of
His
"America's
Biggest Little
Band"

Now!
Offers You the
Biggest and Best
Band of
His Entire
Musical
Career

LAWRENCE WELK

*Plus!*
SUPERHUMAN
Instrumental
Performance Acts
Rendered by the
Accredited Originators
Thereof

— ADDRESS ALL COMMUNICATIONS TO —
MIDDLEWEST BROKERAGE CORPORATION
GENERAL OFFICE
· YANKTON, SOUTH DAKOTA ·

CENTRAL SHOW PRINTING CO.     MASON CITY IOWA

Welk used his popularity at the radio station to promote his band's appearances at dances in the area. When attendance at the dances was sparse, Welk would dance with some of the ladies. He passed out samples of Honolulu Fruit Gum until dance hall managers objected because people tended to discard the gum on the dance floor.

Here we see "Bad Bill" Goodrich, at the piano, with Gurney's Sunshine Cord Tire Orchestra. Members included, from left to right, Harvey Nelson, John Matuska, Zeke Stout, Charley Steinbach, and Jada Wyman.

One of the most popular groups featured on WNAX from the late 1920s until 1940 was the Rosebud Kids. They were the children of Oscar and Sarah Kosta, who came to Yankton from the Rosebud Country of South Dakota. From left to right are Margaret at the piano, violinist George, Harlen with the bass horn, singer Waneta, and Alice at the drums, with their parents behind them.

The Rosebud Kids traveled many evenings in this specially built "stretch" Buick to perform concerts in the area. Bedding in the vehicle enabled the children to sleep on the way home so they could attend school in the morning.

WNAX produced shows especially for children in their first years of broadcasting. Esther Smith, known as Aunt Esther, encouraged children to send pictures to her. Smith and Harry Seils were one of many couples married on the air over WNAX in the 1930s.

Rev. Denton E. Cleveland presented religious programming for WNAX, uniting his listeners into the non-denominational United Church of America. His motto was "All Christians are striving for the same eternal home." Since he was not paid by the station for his services, he asked for free will gifts from his listeners to continue broadcasting.

Herbert Lemke sang his sacred songs in German, a language understood by many of the listeners. Yankton College student Hazel Olson (who later married George B. German) accompanied him on the piano for two weekly 6:00 a.m. shows. D. B. Gurney soon hired her to accompany many more entertainers. From 1928 through 1930, she worked from early morning until midnight for $3 a week until she quit to get married.

George B. German came to WNAX as a Cowboy Balladeer in 1928. He became famous for his song "The Strawberry Roan" and his fictitious dog "Shep." He is featured on the cover of this book of cowboy and mountain ballads.

This is the Gurney Building at Second and Capitol Streets, with employees of Gurney Seed and Nursery Company in front, each one "striving to please you." The WNAX broadcasting studio was moved in 1927 from the home of D. B. Gurney to the third floor of this building. An antenna was strung between two 60 foot towers near the building. The signal reached 500 miles. WNAX became an immediate success across the Northern Plains where people lived in relative isolation.

On the first floor of Gurney Seed and Nursery Company's building was the Sunshine Grocery Store. The seed and nursery company filled the second floor. The third floor featured a "mall" of small shops (barber, beauty salon, clothing store, jewelry store, restaurant, photo studio, and paint and auto departments) and the studio of WNAX. On Sundays, hundreds of cars parked as near to the building as possible.

Live radio programs were broadcast from this glass-enclosed room on the third floor of the Gurney building, accessible by use of a large rope freight elevator. By the end of 1927, WNAX was broadcasting at 1,000 watts from 7:00 a.m. to 6:00 p.m. daily. They received their dial position of 570 on November 11, 1928.

Visitors came to the Gurney building to shop and to watch live performances being broadcast. On rare days when the audience was small, some of the entertainers would phone their spouses to "come down with the kids."

Ivar Nelson and Harry Seils, government licensed radio engineers, are shown with the transmitter in 1930. In 1932, the station joined the Columbia Broadcasting System, allowing listeners to receive national programming as well as local talent.

Here are musicians Eddie (left) and Jimmie Dean who advertised Sunshine Coffee on their radio program. It cost 35¢ a pound, or $6.40 for 20 pounds, and was sent out C.O.D. If customers were not satisfied with the product, they could return the unused portion for a full refund.

This radio wedding took place on February 12, 1929, in the studios of WNAX. From left to right are Jada Wyman, best man; Bill Goodrich and his new wife; and Naomi Burling, bridesmaid. Dozens of such weddings were performed over the air. Gurneys also sponsored weddings in their peony fields north of Yankton. Emma Hall and Richard Witkop were married in 1932 in an airplane as it flew over the Missouri River, as winners of a contest sponsored by WNAX.

Evelyn (Stewart) and Elmer Zimmerman both worked in the Gurney "mall." Evelyn worked in the restaurant, and Elmer worked in an auto parts store. They enjoyed watching broadcasts of WNAX programs whenever they could. Even though they were not married on the air, they had this wedding picture taken at the Richards Photographic Studio, one of the many stores in the Gurney "mall."

Gurneys used WNAX to help people during the Depression of the 1930s. D. B. Gurney contacted the president of Standard Oil and asked him to lower gas prices for farmers, threatening to sell cheaper gas himself. Standard Oil telegraphed back, "Tell Gurney to go to hell. He's only bluffing." In three days, Gurney opened the first of 578 "Fair Price" gas stations in the five-state area. He advertised over the air as well as on this sign on their building.

This building, built in 1932 across the street from Gurney's nursery building, housed the first Fair Price gas station. In addition to their special blend of "alky" gas (gas blended with alcohol made from corn), they sold tires, spark plugs, batteries, oil, and antifreeze.

This road map advertised the WNAX Fair Price Service Stations. People throughout the region became familiar with the green and white gas pumps at the stations. During a special sale promotion in 1933, 4-ply tires sold for $4.95. Truck tires started at $14.95.

A. H. Bane and his niece Patty Bane are shown standing by a gas pump at a WNAX gas station in Moorhead, Minnesota. Gas sold for as little as 17¢ a gallon. Farmers who had been hit hard by the drought and depression of the 1930s brought cans and barrels to the stations to fill and take home for use in their farm machines.

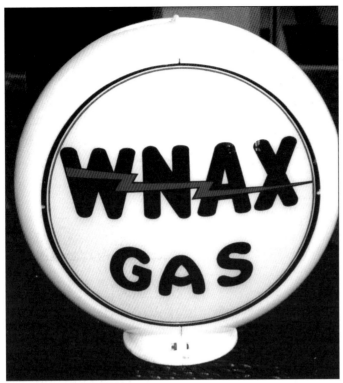

The globes on WNAX gas pumps became the symbol of quality and service at a fair price. Gurneys hosted annual conventions of their Fair Price gas station owners during the approximately 10 years the stations were in existence. The owners attended seminars while their families were entertained with concerts and "sound" movies. The two day events ended with a banquet, featuring D. B. Gurney as toastmaster, followed by a dance.

This restored WNAX gas station was moved to the Pioneer Auto Show and Antique Town in Murdo, South Dakota, from Vivian, South Dakota. Kora Lindquist and her brother Norman operated the station. It is one of only two buildings used for WNAX gas stations known to be in existence at the present time.

# THAT EXTRA PROTECTION
# FOR YOUR MOTOR....

## AND FOR YOUR POCKETBOOK

*Tune to WNAX, Yankton, South Dakota, for the WNAX Gasoline Programs, featuring the Sod Busters from Bar Nothin' Ranch, led by Uncle Ezree Hawkins.*

WNAX Fair Price Gasoline has been designed for America's fine automobiles and for the particular American motorist. The driver's plea for a better motor fuel—a more volatile product—a cleaner burning gasoline has been answered with a premium product commanding a non-premium, or low fair price . . . WNAX Gasoline.

Worthy citizens of the Northwest will always remember the fight of WNAX for fair prices—the organization of the "Affiliated WNAX Fair Price Stations" and the consequent reduction in the price of petroleum products.

Today, as in the past, WNAX Stations stand as sentinels—as guards against former high exorbitant prices. Because of their services, surely they are deserving of your support and patronage.

Drive into your WNAX Station today—fill your car with WNAX Fair Price Products.

# WNAX FAIR PRICE GASOLINE
## AT YOUR NEAREST
# WNAX FAIR PRICE SERVICE STATION

Because of advertisements over WNAX and special promotions, which included giving gas with other purchases, the Fair Price gas stations flourished throughout the 1930s. Then pressure from major oil companies, lack of surplus crops to make alcohol to blend with the gas, the sale of the radio station, and the onset of World War II led to their closing.

# COMMON SENSE

A Monthly Magazine Devoted to the Interests of the Northwest

APRIL, 1932

*Published By*

THE HOUSE OF GURNEY, Inc.

Yankton, South Dakota

*The Party of "The Interrupted Wedding"*
*Oscar Fiddlepoop vs. Miranda Hawkins*

WNAX published a widely circulated magazine called Common Sense, edited by John Peter DePagter, during the 1930s. It featured stories about WNAX radio personalities, articles on many subjects, advertisements for the products WNAX sold over the air, and a classified ad page. On this cover, Oscar Kosta, father of the Rosebud Kids, and known on WNAX as "Oscar Fiddlepoop," plays the part of a bride in a mock wedding.

# "BETTER BUTTER BALLADS"

THE CHORE BOYS

This book of lyrics sung to familiar melodies was published in the early 1930s as part of the Gurneys' efforts to keep oleomargarine from replacing butter on their listeners' tables. With the thought that "A battle is half won if the soldiers are singing," WNAX urged its listeners to go about their daily business singing these songs promoting the use of butter. It was one of many ways WNAX supported agriculture, the most important business in their listening area.

Roy Eastman, known as "Harmonica Dutch," was pictured in the *Better Butter Ballads* book put out by WNAX. The book contained 33 songs, including "O Du Lieber Butterschen," written in German.

Charles Steinbach played xylophone and drums for various WNAX musical groups. This picture is from the *Better Butter Ballads* book. It included such songs as "My Dairy Cow," sung to the tune of "My Maryland," and "Butter Days Are Here Again," sung to the tune of "Happy Days Are Here Again."

Gurneys built this transmitter building five miles east of Yankton near Mission Hill in 1936. It contained the latest modern conveniences, such as a window air conditioner and flush toilets in the upstairs apartment where the engineer and his family lived. The transmitter was on the first floor. Gurneys invited guests to lavish parties on the beautifully landscaped grounds surrounding the building, newly planted in this picture.

Chief engineer Cliff Todd, who came to WNAX in 1930, stands beside the station automobile at the Gurney Nursery building. He was the first engineer to work in the new transmitter building. His staff included 10 engineers: five in the transmitter building, three in the WNAX studios in Yankton, and two at the station's studios in Sioux City.

These engineers worked for WNAX in the mid-1930s. From left to right, they are (first row) Myron Lowery, unidentified, Duke Woods, and Bud Soverngen; (second row) Warren Bailey, Leonard Lange, Stan Whitman, and Cliff Todd.

Engineer Bob Ray, shown here with his wife Luella, moved into the upstairs apartment of the transmitter building with his family in 1939. Bob, a ham radio operator, helped people contact family members serving in the army during World War II. The Ray family lived in the transmitter house until 1964.

George Thompson was caretaker of the WNAX transmitter building and grounds when this picture was taken in 1945. Ornate flower beds, vast green lawns, fruit and shade trees, as well as a state-of-the-art barbecue grill made this "America's most beautifully landscaped transmitter ground," a visible testament to the success of the radio station begun by Al Madson and Chan Gurney so many years before.

# Two

# FACES BEHIND THE VOICES

Chan Gurney's use of WNAX airtime in his bid for a U.S. Senate seat in 1938 without giving equal time to his opponent, Tom Berry, led to a complaint filed with the Federal Communications Commission. As a result, the station's broadcast license was not renewed that year. The station was then purchased by the Des Moines Register and Tribune Company for $170,000. The new owners set up one of the first full-time farm departments with Chuck Worcester as Farm Director, established a news department, and modernized the offices and studios. Live music programs continued until 1955. The new owners opened an additional studio in the Orpheum Building in Sioux City, Iowa, in 1939, where the Central Public Markets program originated. By this time, the station was operating at a power of 5,000 watts during the daytime and 1,000 watts at night. Listeners to WNAX enjoyed a variety of shows from national networks as well as local talent. The voices of these personalities gave rural areas a window on the world and became familiar and beloved to them. This photograph shows Chan Gurney giving a campaign speech from the porch of his parents' house.

A controversy surrounded the purchase of WNAX by Gardner Cowles Jr., shown here, of the Des Moines Register and Tribune Company. The purchase was approved shortly after Cowles had lunch with Pres. Franklin Roosevelt, who had appointed most of the members of the FCC. Cowles became president of WNAX's licensee.

Kate Smith shared her songs with radio audiences on Fridays at 7:00 p.m. Bing Crosby could be heard every weekday at 2:15 p.m. Other famous singers included Dinah Shore and Frank Sinatra. Sunday Evening Party, American Melody Hour, Your Hit Parade, and Great Moments in Music added more hours of musical entertainment. (Courtesy of the Academy of Motion Picture Arts and Sciences.)

On Tuesdays, at 8:00 p.m., people tuned in to hear the famous Guy Lombardo Orchestra. Other nationally known bands and orchestras that could be heard over WNAX included Sammy Kaye, the New York Philharmonic, and Andre Kostelanetz. (Courtesy of Guy Lombardo Music Centre and Friends of Lombardo.)

Soap operas became popular early afternoon diversions for busy rural women, most of whom did not work outside their homes. One of the most popular shows was *Life Can be Beautiful* starring Alice Reinhart, shown in this photograph. Other soap operas included *Our Gal Sunday*, *The Romance of Helen Trent*, *Portia Faces Life*, *Judy and Jane*, *Ma Perkins*, and *Young Doctor Malone*. Most of these programs ran for 15 minutes with time allowed midway for commercials.

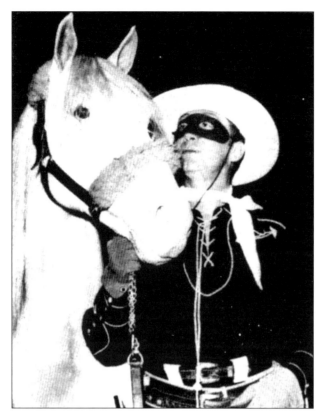

The Lone Ranger was broadcast at 6:30 p.m. on Monday, Wednesday, and Friday and appealed to grown-ups and children. Brace Beemer, who played the part of the Lone Ranger, came to Yankton for WNAX's Midwest Farmers Day in 1944. Other regularly broadcast shows included *The Goldbergs*, *I Love A Mystery*, *The Judy Canova Show*, *Burns and Allen*, *The Adventures of the Thin Man*, *Radio Reader's Digest*, *Inner Sanctum*, *The Aldrich Family*, *Lum and Abner*, and *Lux Radio Theatre*.

*Terry and the Pirates*, a favorite of children, was broadcast daily at 5:15 p.m. Other children's shows included *Let's Pretend*, *Jack Armstrong*, *Quiz Kids*, and *Children's Chapel*.

Larry O'Malley (left) joined his father Happy Jack O'Malley to provide music for WNAX listeners. Larry played the guitar in several musical groups and occasionally played and sang by himself. He started at WNAX in 1943, left for the service in 1945, returned to the station in 1946, and stayed for three years. He returned again in the 1950s to play with the Missouri Valley Barn Dance group.

Here we see, from left to right, Billy Dean, Happy Jack O'Malley, Eddie Texel, and Larry O'Malley entertaining in 1947.

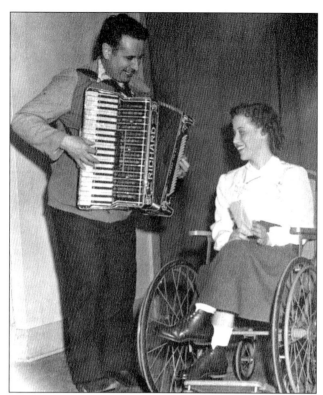

Dick Klasi is shown playing his accordion for Janet Seiler. Klasi, whose nickname was "Noodle Soup," was known for his yodeling and was much enjoyed by the WNAX audiences.

Cora Deane was Dick Klasi's wife and also entertained over WNAX.

Judy (left) and her sister Jennie Herrell formed the group known as Judy, Jen, and George with Judy's husband George Arthur. They broadcast three live 15-minute shows daily from 1949 to 1951. Their repertoire included Western ballads, sacred numbers, and folk songs.

George Arthur was part of the group know as Judy, Jen, and George.

Billy Dean was one of the well-known Western singers on WNAX.

Ben and Jessie Mae Norman sang hymns, Western ballads, and folk tunes on their daily early morning show.

Ben Norman teamed up with Quarantine Brown to send out greetings from WNAX on this postcard in 1953.

Ben Norman  Quarantine Brown.

Hope you're as happy as we all

Here at W.N.A.X. – 570

This group, known as the Westernairs, featured, from left to right, Eddie Johnson, Mel Carson, and Lou Prohut. The group received many fan letters during their years at WNAX (1949–1951). One letter from a satisfied farmer assured them that the cows gave more milk when they sang a particular song. Lou Prohut went on to become a nationally known accordion player on the *Breakfast Club* radio show in Chicago.

45

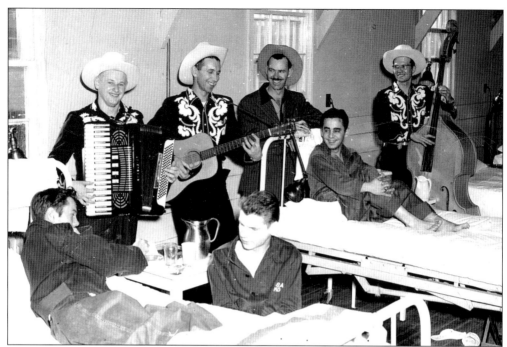

Here we see Lou Prohut and his accordion, along with, from left to right, Eddie Johnson, Billy Dean, and Mel Carson entertaining soldiers at a hospital in Weaver, South Dakota.

Entertainers from WNAX traveled to towns around the five-state area each Saturday night after gas rationing was lifted following World War II to present the WNAX Missouri Valley Barn Dance show, one of the most popular broadcasts the station aired. In addition to providing a variety of musical acts, they included the humor of "Grandpa Windpenny," portrayed by announcer Lloyd (Grant) Reedstrom, shown at the far right of this photograph.

In this 1949 photograph of the Missouri Valley Barn Dance crew, announcers Bob Hill and Lloyd (Grant) Reedstrom are kneeling in the front row. From left to right, the rest are (second row) Lee Jones, Lou Prohut, Mel Carson, Eddie Johnson (the Westernairs), Judy Arthur, Happy Jack O'Malley, Rex Hayes, Jennie Herrell, Bert Dunham, Billy Dean, Jessie Mae and Ben Norman, and Leo Fortin; (third row) Homer Schmidt, Tuffy Dale, Eddie Texel, Lynn Edwards, and Russ Luft.

Listeners to WNAX enjoyed the *Dinner Bell Roundup* show each weekday at noon. Entertainers on the show included, from left to right, (first row) Ben and Jessie Mae Norman, Betty and Marge Carson; (second row) Willie Pierson, Cora Deane, and Dick Klasi; (third row) Harold Arp, Eddie Texel, Marian Matthews, Rex Hays, Larry O'Malley, and "Happy Jack" O'Malley. The show included music, livestock market reports, news, and broadcasts from farm homes.

Beginning at 1:00 p.m. and lasting for two hours, the *Sunday Get-together* featured many of the people who entertained on other shows throughout the week and at the Missouri Valley Barn Dance shows. These programs continued until the 1960s.

Homer Schmidt    Keith Eide    Lynn Edwards    Eddie Texel

Billy Dean    Bill Tonyan    Rex Hays    Fred Burgi

The most popular band on WNAX was the Bohemian Band which broadcast their music from 1939 to 1955 each evening, Monday through Friday, at 6:15. They played waltzes, polkas, and schottisches. The members at the time this photograph was taken were, from left to right, Billy Dean, Homer Schmidt, Bill Tonyan, Keith Eide, Rex Hays, Lynn Edwards, Eddie Texel, and Fred Burgi. Other musicians played in the band at various times.

Marion Matthews played the piano, organ, and novochord. Her favorite instrument was the Hammond Electric Organ at the WNAX studios. She played tunes that were favorites of her listeners. Marion also played with the Bohemian Band.

# Welcome! to

## MENU

### Suggestions:
#### a la Schottische and Waltz

Holzauction                    Saturday Night
  Laughing Blacksmith             Where Is My Youth
    At The Old Village Barn         Forget Me Not
      Blue Eyes                       Silver Lake
        Red Handkerchief                No Vrat Do Vlasti
          Helenka                         Falling Leaf
            Rheinlander                     Zlata Mati

                  Johann Po Snippen

ALL ITEMS FREE: SUBSTITUTIONS AT NO ADDITIONAL COST.

*Please Applaud when Served*

THE STROLLERS

CHECK YOUR CARES AT THE COUNTER

# Caf

## LI

## BO

THE WNAX
*An 8-cou*

Let us watch your troubles

## Polkas:

Happy Go Lucky
  Hot Stuff
    Pilsen
      Dancing Shoes
        Jolly Fellows
          Little Pet (Maly-Ma
            Marching Mice

NOT
RESPONSIBLE
FOR
CORNY LICKS

This brochure advertised the versatility of the Bohemian Band in a humorous way. The band played in ballrooms across the region and recorded music for national distribution.

**One-til-two**
## SATURDAY
### AFTERNOON

TLE

HEMIA

THE TWO-TON TRIO

## Vocal Appetizers:

| | |
|---|---|
| Nana Nana | Rock and Rye Polka |
| Pivo Cerveno | Koline Koline |
| Swiss Boy | Bye Bye Blackbird |
| Muziky-Muziky | Ding Dong Polka |
| Skirt Waltz | Green is Green |

IF OUR MENU DOESN'T INCLUDE YOUR FAVORITE MUSICAL DISH—
REMEMBER—WE'RE FAMOUS FOR SPECIAL REQUESTS

*The management reserves the right to enjoy this hour as much as the customers!*

MIAN BAND

*cal treat*

see that they steal away.

**ing Hot**

Oneta
Clover Leaf
Barn Swallow
Village Tavern
Jirka a Pepik
Heda
Clarinet

COME
IN OVERALLS
WE'LL SUIT YOU!

## THE BOHEMIAN BAND HAS
## ALWAYS CATERED TO
## SPECIAL PARTIES

*(Inquiries Invited)*

Take a case of happiness along—no deposit required.

We're the *Bohemian* Band but we can sing in seven languages!

*The most unique cafe in the midwest — all orders filled without charge*

# WNAX — 570 on your dial — Yankton and Sioux City

The brochure highlighted the many types of music the Bohemian Band played. Printed on back was the current daily schedule for WNAX programming.

Rex Hayes played clarinet, saxophone, and flute with several of the WNAX musical groups, including the Ramblers and the Bohemian Band, which he also directed. He was part of the Stump Us Boys, who attempted to play any song requested by listeners, and he sang in a gospel quartet. He served the station as musical director and librarian, cataloging the vast collection of records and sheet music. He was associated with WNAX for about four decades.

Lloyd (Grant) Reedstrom began announcing for WNAX in 1948. He and the other news announcers made sure local farm issues were covered as well as national and international events. In the mid-1950s, WNAX maintained a telephonic recorder so they could broadcast transcriptions direct from the scene of any major news event.

Here we see Lloyd (Grant) Reedstrom as he portrayed Grandpa Windpenny over the air and at the Missouri Valley Barn Dance shows. Grant was so convincing in that characterization that when he was hospitalized for surgery, adoring fans sent over 800 get well messages to Grandpa Windpenny, some of them commenting on how hard it must be for such an "old person" to go through with an operation.

The WNAX announcers became celebrities in their own right. Chris (Mack) McMenamy, who became Farm Service Director in 1941, often attended national farm meetings. His interviews with farmers were sometimes picked up by national networks. His *Farm News* show featured national and regional farm news, information on the latest farming practices, weather forecasts, and market estimates.

George B. German headed the farm department from 1941 until 1975. *RFD with George B.* became one of the most widely-enjoyed programs on the station. German wrote articles for WNAX's *Common Sense* magazine. After retiring from WNAX, he became curator of Yankton's Dakota Territorial Museum. He was a member of the South Dakota Cowboy Hall of Fame and the South Dakota Broadcaster Hall of Fame. He died in 1991.

**WARREN KOESTER**

**RAY SWITZER**

Farmers in the listening area depended on daily market reports given by Don Cunningham (center) at 12:15 p.m. His reports told farmers and ranchers about the future of their products so they could market them most profitably. He stayed with the station for 20 years. Warren Koester (left) and Ray Switzer (right) reported with Cunningham from the Sioux City stockyards.

Arthur J. Smith (left) managed the Sioux City studio as well as doing a newscast. He had been "Jiggs" to Wynn Speece's "Maggie" when they both worked at a radio station in Des Moines, Iowa. He hired her for her first job at WNAX. He was program manager from 1937 to 1942. He covered the dedication of the Roosevelt head on Mount Rushmore for CBS in 1939 and worked with Edward R. Murrow on Missouri River coverage.

Whitey Larson was one of the favorite newscasters on WNAX with his neighborly style of speaking. He did the Sunset Edition of the news each evening. On Sunday evenings, he would tell the ladies listening to soak their laundry if the weather forecast indicated a sunny Monday. After he finished the late edition of the news at 10:15 p.m., pilots flying overhead would see lights going out across he countryside.

Bob Hill was a small man, but listeners knew him for his deep voice. He was news director for WNAX for almost 40 years beginning in 1947. In winter, he would make phone calls to people in the surrounding area before going on the air so he could update the listeners on conditions. He often traveled to other towns with the Missouri Valley Barn Dance crew, arriving back in Yankton just in time to do the announcing for *Sunday Get-Together* program at the station.

Bob "Uncle Bob" Hill and Mary "Aunt Mary" Krause broadcast a children's show *called Rhyme and Riddle Time* each Saturday morning. It included a fictional dog named Squeaky. They encouraged their listeners to send in letters and received hundreds of them. They are shown here, from left to right, in 1949 with the Westernairs, (first row) Eddie Johnson, unidentified child, Lou Prohut, and Mel Carson; (second row) Mary Krause and Bob Hill.

Don O'Brien was a sportscaster for the station. He did Big 10 and Big 6 football games as well as local games. WNAX started broadcasting area sports events as early as 1927, when they aired the state basketball tournament from the Corn Palace in Mitchell, South Dakota.

The Ranch Girls, Carolyn Osterberg (left) and Muriel Fredrickson, entertained on many of the live broadcasts on WNAX from 1951 to 1956. Originally from Blue Island, Illinois, these cousins were brought to Yankton by their agent.

The *Stump Us Gang* was a popular show for many years. People called in with song titles to see if they could stump the group of musicians who tried to play the songs. Shown here in the 1950s are, from left to right, announcer Bob King, Lynn Edwards, Keith Eide, Eddie Texel, Rex Hays, and Bill Tonyan.

These announcers, known as the voices of WNAX, are, from left to right, Al Constant, "Jolly" Joe Martin, Cap Mally, and Mal Murray.

Roland (Pete) Peterson broadcast over WNAX from 1939 until 1970. He enjoyed getting to meet his listeners who knew him by his soft baritone voice. During his years with the station, he worked in all departments from promotion and production to farm reporting. For many years, he was farm safety program director. He received the DeKalb "Oscar in Agriculture" award in 1969 as the nation's most dedicated farm broadcaster.

Robert Tincher was named General Manager of WNAX in 1938, after Gurneys sold the station to Gardner Cowles Jr.'s Des Moines Register and Tribune Company. He became vice president at the station in 1946.

Herb Howard came to WNAX in 1947 as program director and announcer for such shows as the *Sunday Get-Together*, *Paraland Pennfield*, and the *Circle B Dude Ranch Show*. He was successful in increasing the listening audience of the station by giving the farm audience what they wanted to hear.

Don Inman was station manager and also worked in sales and promotion. He was typical of many employees of WNAX who worked at more than one job while at the station. It is not possible to include every person who worked at the station over the years, but the efforts of each one helped to make WNAX the success it came to be.

# *Three*

# BIG AGGIE LAND

Radio station WNAX provided not only entertainment via its broadcasts, but also special events for its listeners. Pancake Days and Midwest Farmer Day were two popular examples. People came by the thousands to Yankton or to other locations where the events were held and enjoyed meeting the people behind the voices they had come to know. At the 1928 Watermelon Day, thousands came to enjoy free watermelon and observe the demonstration of a radio controlled airplane whose pilot responded to commands given from a microphone in the radio studio. Because agriculture was the most important industry in the five-state region, many of the special events centered around programs designed to educate and entertain farmers and their families. The announcers who brought market news and weather reports became trusted friends upon whom the farmers could depend when making important decisions. In 1957, WNAX received its seventh consecutive National Farm Safety award, a feat no other radio or television station could match.

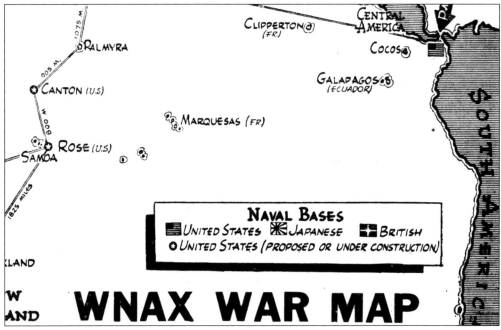

WNAX provided special services during World War II. Within hours after the attack at Pearl Harbor, they offered maps of the Pacific area to their listeners. In five days, 47,000 people wrote for maps. They sold war bonds, furnished entertainers for war bond rallies, and helped people find scarce commodities. Women could order fabrics from the station by specifying what color they wanted.

In the 1940s, when many women had to run farms while their husbands were off fighting in World War II, WNAX introduced this symbol and began to refer to its listening area as "Big Aggie Land." The term referred to "big agriculture."

Coin banks made with the Big Aggie image became popular and are prized by collectors today.

Don Inman (seated), who was in sales for WNAX at the time, and Phil Hoffman, station manager, display a Big Aggie doll.

In 1943, WNAX built a 927-foot-high radio tower beside the transmitter building east of Yankton, near the small town of Mission Hill. Cables were used to lift the upper segments of the tower into place.

Homer Rosser, shown here on the left with chief engineer Cliff Todd, was the construction foreman for the tower project. Rosser represented the Beasley Construction Corporation of Dallas, Texas. He had also supervised the construction of the first WNAX tower at the transmitter site in 1935. Because World War II was being waged at the time the 927-foot tower was built, a federal dispensation for steel to build the tower had to be obtained.

The new tower was the tallest radio tower in the country at that time and was dedicated to Midwest farmers with these words: "In tribute to the typical Midwest farmer who gave unstintingly of his labor, surmounted every obstacle and will continue on the same path that the world may be fed."

TALLEST RADIO STATION IN THE WORLD
WNAX
YANKTON, SO.DAK. J-141

WNAX installed a 5 kilowatt Western Electric transmitter in the power room of the transmitter building. After the completion of the 927-foot tower, the station increased its nighttime power to 5,000 watts. By using all three of the towers at the transmitting location, optimal directional control was obtained. Engineers Cliff Todd (left) and Robert Ray show off their up-to-date equipment.

The dedication of the new tower in 1943 began with speeches by dignitaries at the Yankton College football stadium. Then everyone drove the five miles to the transmitter site for the dedication. It took two hours to make the short trip due to the number of cars. When the last segment of the tower, with a huge American flag attached, reached its destination at the top, 12 balloons containing certificates for saving bonds were released.

As part of the dedication activities, WNAX began its practice of honoring a "typical Midwest farmer" couple chosen from nominees from the five states in the listening area. Thousands of people came to Yankton for these occasions to enjoy a parade, speeches, free pancakes, and entertainment by WNAX musicians. Shown are Mr. and Mrs. John Oeser, Westside, Iowa, who received the honor in 1945.

Aunt Jemima, representative of the company which made the Aunt Jemima pancake mix, came to Yankton in 1945 to serve her famous pancakes during Midwest Farmer Day. The entire community benefited from the event. Hotels were full and main street merchants did a big business. To keep the children from going through the line twice for the free pancakes, servers dipped the child's finger in iodine on their first trip through.

## WNAX MIDWEST FARMER DAY
## 1950
## RESERVED SEAT PASS

This card entitles bearer to ..........*One*.......... seats in the reserved seat section for both afternoon and evening performances during the Midwest Farmer Day finale celebration of the WNAX Farmstead Improvement Program.

## SIOUX CITY AUDITORIUM --- SAT., OCT. 28

(Note: Please retain this card. It will admit to all of the day's activities)

Midwest Farmer Day continued for about 20 years, sometimes lasting up to five days. Many nationally known radio stars attended and performed for the thousands of people who came. As another way of supporting farmers, WNAX started a three-year Farmstead Improvement Program in 1948. Farmers who showed the greatest improvement to their farms during that period of time received $40,000 and other awards.

Marie Killian came to WNAX in 1947 and stayed until 1991. She started as program secretary and moved into the accounting department. During her years at the station, she was also office manager and business manager. When the WNAX building and all its contents were destroyed by fire in 1983, she reconstructed many of the vital records from memory.

Marie Billings, shown here to the left of Marie Killian, was another longtime secretary at WNAX. Friendships among the staff members extended into their private lives. They often gathered for holiday parties and other social events.

Staff members during the 1940s included, from left to right, Cliff Todd, engineer; Roland (Pete) Peterson, announcer; unidentified; Herb Howard, program director; Dick Harris; and Chris Mack, announcer and farm service director. All the members of the staff were invited to the transmitter grounds each summer for an elaborate company picnic. While a variety of meats cooked over the large outdoor grill, those attending played horse shoes, bingo, or other games. Prizes were of exceptional quality, all with the WNAX logo on them.

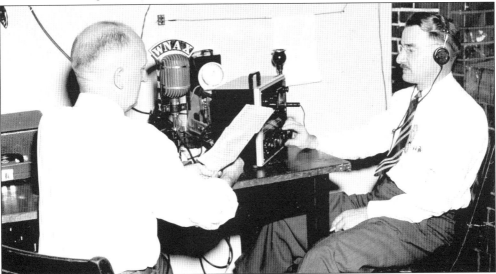

Whitey Larson, announcer (left), and Cliff Todd kept listeners updated on national political conventions in 1944 as part of the station's service to its listeners. In the winter of 1949, when parts of the region received 98 inches of snow, WNAX was often the only contact people had with the outside world. Announcers advised listeners to stamp out emergency messages in the snow, thereby helping rescuers find stranded people.

Beginning in 1950, WNAX sponsored an annual Five-State Bowling Tournament, the largest regional bowling tournament in America. Throughout the history of the event, the station awarded over $500,000 in prizes. Shown here is one of the WNAX teams including, from left to right, Lora Collett, Marie Killian, Dorothy Weimers, Eunice Becker, and Alice Heins.

In 1951, WNAX moved into the Stuelpnagel Building at 319 East Third Street, shown here. The grand opening of the building coincided with the annual Pancake Days festival, extended to three days that year. The building contained two broadcasting studios. Studio B was acoustically perfect and "suspended" to prevent any vibrations from interfering with live broadcasts. WNAX re-affiliated with the CBS network that year after having joined ABC in 1945.

This is Studio A in the Stuelpnagel Building. The *Missouri Valley Barn Dance* and *Sunday Get Together* were two shows broadcast from this studio in front of an audience. The large stage was to be used for telecasts, should they ever originate in Yankton.

These people are looking at pictures of WNAX entertainers at the station's booth set up for the *Sports and Builders Show*. It was held in the Sioux City Auditorium in April 1952.

Robert R. Tincher (left), general manager of WNAX, received copies of a documentary tape recording a program on Missouri River floods. WNAX produced the program to promote the building of dams after a series of disastrous floods. Presenting the tapes in May of 1952 is Dr. Luther Evans, the librarian of Congress.

Art Smith interviews Bob Hope at a polio benefit program held in Sioux City in 1952.

WNAX used this unusual display to touch off their Memorial Day safety campaign on May 30, 1952. It was set up on U.S. Highway 81 leading north out of Yankton.

These educators toured the building on Business Education Day on April 15, 1952. From left to right are Dr. Harry Savage and Rosamond Hall, Yankton College; local public school teachers Sarah Goodburn, Marguerite Kahoutek, and Myrtle Anderson; Dr. Evelyn Hoff, Yankton College; local teachers Mary Anderson, Laura Croston, Wyonne Kurth, and Mary Anne Noren; Gertrud Seidel, exchange teacher from Germany; and Sisters Josita and Michelline from Sacred Heart School.

LLOYD GRANT

JACK BRUCE

JACK HANNON

BILL JOHNSON

Staff members at the studio in the 1950s included, from left to right, Lloyd (Grant) Reedstrom, Jack Hannon, Bill Johnson, and Bruce (Jack Bruce) Krause. When WNAX moved from the Gurney building into their new studios on Third Street, Johnson introduced Whitey Larson's news broadcast in the Gurney building, then rushed to the new building in time to introduce Les Davis's sports cast from there 15 minutes later.

Bruce (Jack Bruce) Krause came to WNAX in 1948. He did a show called *The Bandwagon* and, as "Jumping Jack Bruce," he emceed the *Missouri Valley Barn Dance Show* and kept it moving along at a happy, fast pace.

Les Davis did a sports broadcast called *Today in the World of Sports*, Monday through Saturday at 10:15 p.m. His background as an outstanding athlete, coach, and athletic director had earned him a nationwide reputation as a sports authority. He directed the WNAX Five-State Bowling Tournament in the 1950s and 1960s, the world's largest regional bowling tournament at the time and the largest sports event ever sponsored by an American radio station.

Members of the WNAX staff dressed in period costumes to help celebrate the centennial of the city of Yankton in 1961. From left to right are Carol Shuff, Marie Billings, Marie Killian, and Amanda Johnson.

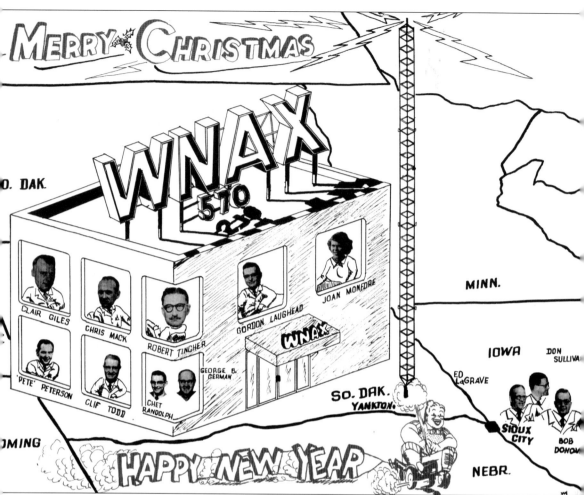

WNAX sent out this Christmas card in the late 1940s. Members of the staff are pictured in the drawing. Featured are two symbols of the station: the radio tower and Big Aggie. From left to right, they are (first row) Pete Peterson, Cliff Todd, Chet Randolph, and George B. German; (second row in "windows") Clair Giles, Chris Mack, Robert Tincher, Gordon Laughead, and Joan Monfore. In the right corner are Ed LaGrave, Don Sullivan, and Bob Donovan.

Wynn Speece, shown here, replaced Susan Taylor as the women's director. She started her *Neighbor Lady* show on July 14, 1941, and continued broadcasting until December 23, 2005. Her daily visit, which included giving recipes for her listeners to copy, became an important part in the lives of isolated farm women throughout the five-state region.

Listeners became familiar with the names of the engineering staff because announcers often referred to them during programming, for example, when they gave the temperature which was reported from the transmitter site. Myron "Monk" Lowry, shown here, was transmitter supervisor.

Engineer Leonard Lange is shown sitting at the controls in the transmitter building.

Engineer Bob Ray (left) lived in the apartment over the transmitter rooms with his family for 25 years. His son, Stan Ray, Yankton mortician, has many happy memories of growing up at the site. He remembers that his mother would signal his dad to come upstairs from the transmitter rooms on the first floor for coffee by thumping three times on the floor of the apartment. At right is engineer Leonard Lange.

Engineer John Willson often traveled with Wynn Speece when she took her *Neighbor Lady* show on the road. He was with WNAX from 1940 to 1970. He is shown here with his wife Arvilla.

Ed Gurney was an engineer for the station. He was the nephew of D. B. Gurney.

The engineers who worked at WNAX during the 1940s, 1950s, and 1960s, and their families, became close friends. Most were about the same age and were hired about the same time. These men, all engineers at WNAX posed, each with their first-born child, in 1939. From left to right are Leonard Lange and daughter Jean Ann, Robert Ray and son Stan, Maurice Mitchell and daughter Patricia, and Stanley Whitman and daughter Portia.

# "MY DAY"

THIS IS MY DAY. GOD HAS GIVEN ME THIS DAY TO USE AS I WILL. I CAN WASTE IT . . . OR USE IT FOR GOOD. WHAT I DO TODAY IS VERY IMPORTANT, BECAUSE I'M EXCHANGING A DAY OF MY LIFE FOR IT. WHEN TOMORROW COMES, THIS DAY WILL BE GONE FOREVER, LEAVING SOMETHING IN ITS PLACE.

MAY GOD, WHO GAVE ME THIS DAY, ALSO GIVE ME THE WISDOM TO KNOW HOW TO LIVE IT . . . TO BE DIRECTED TO ADD GOOD TO IT . . . NOT EVIL. MAY THE LIFE WHICH HE ALSO GAVE ME BE WELL SPENT FOR THIS DAY.

Bob Hill recorded this prayer, which was read over WNAX at 5:00 a.m. daily for many years.

Cowles Broadcasting sold WNAX to Peoples Broadcasting Corporation in 1957. Red Owl Stores Incorporated bought WNAX on September 1, 1965, through its subsidiary, Area Wide Communications Incorporated. They announced the purchase in this issue of the *Owlmanac*, which was published for all current and retired employees of Red Owl Stores Incorporated.

WNAX was a unifying force in the Northern Plains in the years when people were still relatively isolated. The staff of the station knew what its listeners needed to hear to keep them in touch and up to date. They sent out yearly program guides featuring photographs of the staff and network entertainers as well as the daily scheduling of programs. This one, now a collector's item, was sent in 1945.

# *Four*

# YOUR NEIGHBOR LADY

It is 3:30 p.m. The melodic strains of "Come Back to Sorrento" swell across the air waves. Women all over the five-state WNAX listening area stop whatever they are doing, grab a cup of coffee, a pencil, and a pad of paper and sit down, likely for the first time since washing the noontime dishes. The melody fades away, replaced by a cheery voice saying, "And hello there, good friends!" Each listener feels as though she has been greeted personally by Wynn Speece, the Neighbor Lady. Speece's program of friendly housewife-to-housewife visiting, the recipes and helpful hints she gave, and her offers to send out products she had checked to guarantee their value, became a daily ritual in the lives of thousands of women. Letters poured in from them wanting to share their lives with her or to order the products she advertised. When she traveled into the surrounding communities to do cooking shows, huge crowds waited to meet her. It all began in 1941, and, with variations over the years, continued to 2005. Wynn Speece became Your Neighbor Lady, a phenomenon in broadcasting history.

Wynn (Hubler) Speece's first day on the job at WNAX was unsettling to her. After the ride to the third floor studios, past a grocery store and plant nursery, on an open-sided freight elevator operated with a rope, she discovered her office had to be entered through a hole in the floor. But she persevered and is shown here with Art Smith, celebrating her first year at WNAX. She had met Smith when they both worked at a station in Des Moines, Iowa, before coming to Yankton.

Barbara (Bates) Gunderson, at right, worked in the continuity office with Wynn Speece, where they wrote commercials and maintained the daily advertising log. They became immediate friends and decided to share an apartment. Occasionally, Speece played small parts on the *Flying Arrow Show,* where Bates played "Ma Brown." Bates referred to Speece as her "neighbor lady" on those shows, a name that became famous when Speece used it for her own show later.

Sometimes Speece broadcast from this WNAX studio in Sioux City. Her first show was *Ways to Win with Wynn Hubler*, a 15 minute show on Saturday mornings to showcase products offered by WNAX advertisers. Speece is seated fourth from the left.

In 1941, Phil Hoffman, station manager, promoted Speece to women's director and increased her air time to 15 minutes daily. He liked the title "Neighbor Lady," which Barbara Bates had originated, so it was used on the show. It was a great success and mail began to pour in. In later years, when she did a longer daily show, it came in by the bag as shown here. At right is a representative from the Katz Advertising Agency which was the national advertising agency for the station.

Due to the great listener response, Wynn Speece's show was moved from 4:30 p.m. to 3:30 p.m. so women could hear the program before their children came home from school. Rural women, many living in isolated areas, eagerly awaited the recipes and the household tips, all presented in Speece's friendly, visiting style.

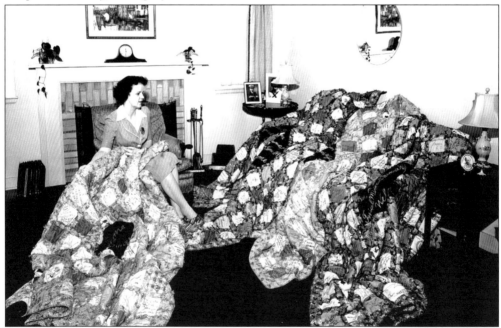

At Midwest Farmer Day in 1943, Speece was presented with six huge quilts her listeners had made by embroidering their names and addresses on five-inch square patches, which were sewn together to make the quilts. One quilt went to a scholarship winner in each of the five states of the immediate listening area, and one was presented to Speece. She still uses it.

Speece met her husband Harry Speece when he was assigned to Yankton College for training as part of the Naval Air Corps V5 Flight Program in World War II. During their courtship, Wynn Speece's mother died, so she moved back to Des Moines, Iowa, to live with her father. Harry Speece had been transferred to a training station near Ottumwa, Iowa. They were able to get together to make wedding plans, and were married on January 3, 1945.

Speece continued to broadcast over WNAX while she and her husband lived in Des Moines. Her listeners were delighted that she was now a married lady, as were most of them. They sent her wedding gifts and wrote letters expressing their gratitude that she had shared this special time with them. As her popularity with her WNAX listeners continued to grow, she and her husband decided to move back to Yankton. Harry Speece worked at WNAX as the marketing director from 1947 to 1949.

Wynn Speece is shown here with Al Constant, an announcer who occasionally sat in for her when she had to be absent. At one time, he challenged her to a cookie baking contest. He and Speece each baked a batch of peanut butter cookies. The judges, admitting to be biased, were sure that the perfectly round cookies were Speece's and voted for them. They turned out to be Constant's, which resulted in him being declared the WNAX Cookie King, much to his pleasure.

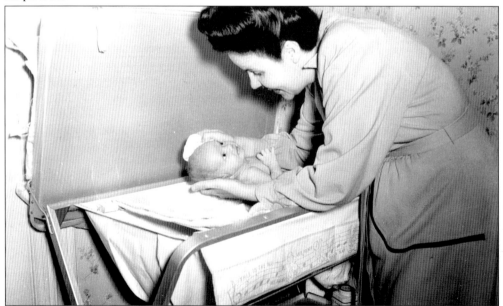

When Speece discovered she was pregnant, she went to Bob Tincher, station manager, to give her resignation. But he suggested she start broadcasting from her home after the baby was born. That setting added a special warmth to the program. As her sons Peter and Todd came along, she shared family moments to the delight of her listeners.

Speece and other station personnel planned Christmas events for several children's institutions in the area. Here she is shown with Governor Sigurd Anderson at the Sioux Falls Crippled Children's Home. WNAX also sponsored an annual Christmas party for the Sioux City Boys and Girls home and St. Mary's Episcopal School for Indian Girls in Springfield, South Dakota. Speece's listeners sent her gifts and money in overwhelming quantities for the parties.

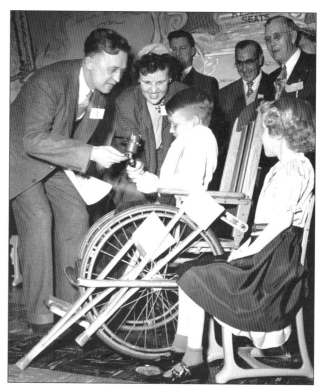

Through the work the Speeces did with the Sioux City Home for Boys and Girls, they became acquainted with Dorothy Gibson. When Gibson turned 16 and had to leave the institution, the Speeces offered her a home with them and regarded her as their daughter. During broadcasts from the Speece home, Gibson kept the younger children from interrupting their mother. From left to right, they are (first row) Todd Speece, Wynn Speece, Dorothy Gibson, and Peter Speece; (second row) Gretchen Speece and Harry Speece.

When Wynn Speece made personal appearances in stores to promote her products, the store owners could count on huge crowds and shelves emptied out by enthusiastic customers. Here she is with A. E. Kapitan at his store in Yankton. She sold more than a quarter of a million orders for plastic "food saver" bags over the air. Her great success prompted many companies to seek her out to promote their products.

As Speece's popularity grew, she was able to choose which products she would advertise. Over the years, she had over 50 sponsors including Red Devil Soot Remover, Swift and Company Lard, Holiday Macaroon Mix, and Fashion Frocks. Here she visits with Elmer Zimmerman while doing an in-store promotion in the Sears store in Yankton.

Speece traveled around the region to make personal appearances on behalf of the products she advertised. She visited her sponsor Hope's Fashion Farm located in Cherokee, Iowa.

Speece enjoyed getting to meet her listeners. She invited them to picnics throughout the area. Women thronged to the events, along with their children and a few husbands. In fact, Speece often got letters from women telling them their husbands enjoyed her show, too, and copied recipes that sounded good to them. She is seated near the center of this picture, wearing a large hat.

In this photograph, Wynn Speece is visiting with her fans in Niobrara, Nebraska, in 1954. Behind her are banners showing some of the many products she advertised.

Speece broadcast from this booth at the Iowa State Fair. Loyal listeners crowded around.

Speece was in great demand as a speaker. Here, she addresses a group in a church basement. She was known for the large hats she wore in a time when women usually wore hats in public.

Terrace Park Dairy, Sioux Falls, became one of Speece's sponsors in the mid-1940s and continued with her throughout her years of broadcasting the *Neighbor Lady Show*. Founders of the dairy, Al and Ozzie Schock, pose with her in front of the home offices of the company.

Early in her broadcast years, Wynn Speece developed the Perfect Menu contest. Each year, she encouraged women to send in recipes for appetizers, entrees, vegetable side dishes, and desserts. From these, she chose a perfect menu, which the winners were invited to help her cook and eat. The day started with a shopping trip to buy the needed groceries, shown here. In 1954, she received 4,496 entries in the contest.

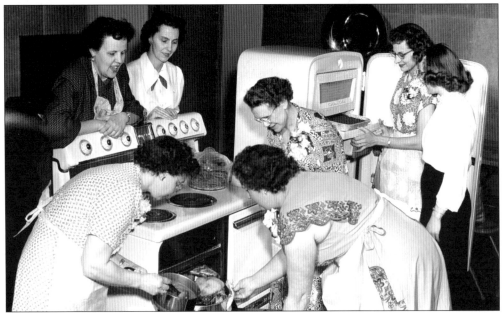

Speece watches as winners of the Perfect Menu cook the food for their prize-winning meal. The women enjoyed getting to know her on a personal basis as they worked together. The contest was televised for a few years when KVTV in Sioux City was owned by the Cowles Broadcasting Company, but Speece did not enjoy the bustle of a video production.

The husbands were invited to participate in eating the Perfect Menu meal with Speece and the contest winners. Many were farm couples who treasured this occasion as a special diversion in their everyday lives. Prizes for winners included, besides the opportunity of working with Speece, automatic percolators, sets of flatware, and other homemaking items.

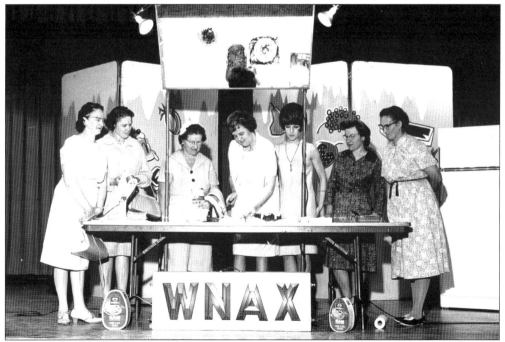

The success of the Perfect Menu contest led to the Kitchen Karnival shows where Speece did cooking demonstrations in various locations for occasions such as fairs, pork or dairy festivals, and farm shows. An overhead mirror helped her audiences see what she was doing on the table.

Doing a traveling cooking show meant Wynn Speece and her staff had to transport all manner of cooking equipment and boxes of ingredients wherever they were to appear. Often Speece used utensils from her own kitchen because she was more familiar with them. Things did not always go smoothly. Sometime essential ingredients were forgotten, appliances malfunctioned, or weather hampered their efforts while doing outdoor demonstrations.

During the late 1950s throughout the 1960s, announcer Norm Hilson joined Speece for a four-hour show each afternoon from Thanksgiving through Christmas Eve. The show, called *Happy Holidays*, featured seasonal music, recipes, readings, and friendly chatter between the two hosts. It became a favorite way for listeners to get into the spirit of the holidays.

Speece knew her listeners would enjoy a collection of the many recipes they had sent her, so she started putting out an annual *Neighbor Lady Book* in 1941 (shown here). She sent a "good deed dollar" to each contributor of an especially thoughtful letter printed in the book. War Savings stamps were awarded for recipes published. In 1945, she began to include pictures of her family as well as pictures sent in by listeners.

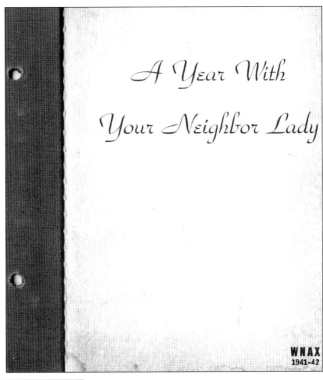

*A Year With Your Neighbor Lady*

WNAX
1941-42

The cost of a Neighbor Lady book rose from 25¢ for the first issue to $1—just enough to cover costs of producing it. The final edition appeared in 1972, and complete sets are now collectors' items. Shown here are Ruth and Ken Melby, Yankton, with the new dishwasher Ruth Melby received for having the prize winning recipe, "Double Cruncher Cookies," in the 1970 book.

As Wynn Speece's daughter Gretchen, shown at left, grew into her teenage years, Speece began to include a five-minute segment called "Teen Talk Time" in her show. It featured discussion of fashions and the fun and frustrations of being a teenager.

Speece was often asked to judge contests. Here we see her sampling cheesecakes at the Sioux Empire Farm Fair in 1955.

Speece judged many queen contests. She included the winners in her broadcasts done on location at the events. Here she introduces the 1969 Pork Queen, Cynthia Long from Olivet, South Dalota, at Viborg, South Dakota, Pork Show.

Speece enjoyed doing interviews, as shown here. Several years later, she conducted one at the 1960 WNAX sponsored National Plowing Contest during the presidential campaigns of Kennedy and Nixon. Speece was to interview Patricia Nixon. An all-day rain had turned the ground to deep mud. Station manager Don Inman pushed Speece through the crowd of 175,000 and lifted her to the stage. She conducted the interview, rain-soaked, with mud-caked shoes. She often wonders what the elegant Patricia Nixon thought.

In 1965, Red Owl Stores bought WNAX. Elmer Smith, shown on the right, became general manager. Radio was changing; few shows were being broadcast live. In 1967, Wynn Speece was asked to stop broadcasting from her home and return to the station to do her shows.

Speece agreed to the return to station broadcasting. Her children were grown (shown in a picture around that time, from left to right, Gretchen, Wynn, husband Harry, Peter, and Todd Speece). No longer did she need to watch through her window for their homecoming from school as she broadcast from her dining room table. Her return to the station marked the end of a unique broadcasting experience for her and her devoted listeners.

In 1970, Speece's show, which had expanded to 50 minutes, was divided into six short shows throughout the day. Although she did not enjoy that format, she realized it was inevitable. The size of her listening audience decreased as farms became larger, diminishing the rural population. Women joined the workforce and were no longer at home to hear her show. In 1973, she did what she thought would be her last *Neighbor Lady Show*. Here she visits with announcer Lyle Hansen.

Speece next worked as marketing director at First Dakota National Bank in Yankton for 10 years. During that time, she did a radio show on station KYNT for the bank. In 1983, she began writing a column for the *Yankton Press and Dakotan* in which she gave recipes and wrote in the style of her former Neighbor Lady broadcasts. This photograph shows her visiting with two longtime listeners, Augusta Simonson (left) and Lucille Thompson, both of Mission Hill, South Dakota.

In 1960, when Wynn Speece was at the height of her popularity, Bob Warren, first from left in the photograph, flew her and two other WNAX personnel to a meeting in Minneapolis. On the way home, ice forced them to land on a country road near Humphrey, Minnesota. A farmer, Mel Simon, shown at the right, took them to his home where his excited wife recognized Speece and gave them a warm and enthusiastic welcome. Harry Speece joined them in this recent reunion photograph.

In 1984, Speece announced in her newspaper column that she would be returning to WNAX with five short programs each week beginning on June 4. Her familiar "Hello there, good friends," prompted many of her former listeners to write telling her how happy they were to have her back. She is shown autographing her biography, written by Jill Karolevitz, third from right, and published in 1987. It prompted Governor George Mickelson to declare July 14, 1987, "Neighbor Lady Day."

Speece received many awards and honors throughout her broadcasting career. In 1959, she received the top award in the "Life Line of America" competition for her promotion of quality food products through her program. At left is the representative from the Grocery Manufacturers of America. At center is Don Sullivan, general manager of WNAX. In 1970, Speece was awarded an Award of Special Merit by Sioux Falls Advertising Club for outstanding presentation on the air.

Wynn and Harry Speece were honored by their hometown by being named Riverboat Days captain and belle at Yankton's yearly summertime celebration in 1986.

In 1992, Wynn Speece received the prestigious Marconi Award as the "Small Market Personality of the Year." She is shown here with Rick Prusator, general manager of WNAX, at the Convention Center in New Orleans where the award was presented.

Speece was selected as Yankton's Citizen of the Year in 1991. She is shown here after being inducted into the South Dakota Hall of Fame in 1995. Gary Owen (right), nationally known announcer and actor, was inducted into the hall of fame the same year.

Speece is shown at the hall of fame banquet with longtime friends, from left to right, Judy Ray, Stan Ray, Joyce Hagen, Dr. Clarence Hagen, and unidentified. She was awarded the distinguished alumna award in 2001 from Drake University, which she had attended.

In 1986, Speece retired from her job at the bank. In 2000, after taping a week's shows for WNAX in the afternoon, she had a heart attack. After being dismissed from the hospital, she was able to tape the next week's shows in time for their broadcast. On July 24, 2001, she was commended on the floor of the U.S. Senate for her 60 years of broadcasting, making her the longest running radio personality in the nation at that time. She is shown doing a broadcast in 2005, at which time she said, "It's a joy for me to be still broadcasting at age 88!"

Wynn Speece received a Doctor of Humane Letters from Mount Marty College, Yankton, on May 8, 2004. College President Dr. James T. Barry (left) and Vice Chairman of the Board of Trustees Denis Fokken (right) bestowed the award. In 2005, she had increased her broadcasting record to 64 years. She was well into her 65th year of broadcasting when she retired on December 23, 2005.

# Five

# THE TRADITION GOES ON

The last third of the 20th century brought changes in personnel and programming at WNAX. The station was purchased in December 1968 by Roy H. Park Broadcasting of The Midwest Incorporated. No longer did entertainers do live shows from the station. By the 1960s, the station was broadcasting "uptempo/easy listening" music. That changed to a country music format in 1971. Farm programming continued to be the major component of the daily shows. Events such as Midwest Farmer Days, Pancake Days, and Neighbor Lady Picnics faded away and were replaced by new promotions in keeping with the modern lifestyles of the listeners. The path to the present day was marked with events inside and outside the studio that made WNAX what it is today—a force that continues to support agriculture. Saga Communications purchased the station in 1996. Its FM station began broadcasting country music as well as news, sports, and weather in early 1991. Both the AM and FM stations are on the air 24 hours each day. This van, dubbed the "Rolling Cornfield," was used to take WNAX personnel to locations where they could do remote broadcasts.

Rex Messersmith was the general manager of the station from 1969 to 1970. He was also program director and worked in the Farm Service Department. Messersmith, George B. German, and Gary Neilan traveled the five-state area gathering information and presenting programs to assist listeners involved in agriculture. Messersmith participated in National Corn Picking Contests, National 4-H Congress, International Livestock Exposition, and National Association of Television and Radio Farm Directors.

Don Weberg, farm director at WNAX from 1968 until 1972, is shown receiving an award from Gary Enright, from the South Dakota Farm Bureau, in 1974. Weberg taught vocational agriculture for several years before becoming a farm broadcaster.

Craighton Knau came to WNAX's farm department in 1956. He covered farm-related events such as the Minimum Tillage Field Day near Madison, South Dakota, in 1966. He produced radio recordings for the American Society of Agricultural Engineers during their annual meetings. He served as president of the National Association of Farm Broadcasters in 1983 and was named to that organization's hall of fame posthumously in 2004.

Russ Bailey worked in sales and promotions in the 1950s and continued into the 1980s. He was also an announcer and served as general manager for a short time.

These announcers are shown as they worked in the WNAX booth at the South Dakota State Fair in 1992. From left to right are Christy Lee, Patty Burry, and Sonja Bailey. Bailey is the daughter of Russ Bailey, former WNAX announcer.

Ed Nelson worked at WNAX for 29 years. He was farm director for 14 years beginning in 1974 until he retired in 1988. He was a member of the National Association of Farm Broadcasters. Nelson enjoyed visiting with his listeners as well as talking with local and national agricultural leaders. He and his fellow farm broadcasters at WNAX helped farmers through difficult times with their optimism and vital informational programs. He died in 2005.

Norm Hilson came to WNAX in 1956 as sports director. He was voted sportscaster of the year five times. He was elected to the North Central Collegiate Conference Hall of Fame as well as the SDSU Hall of Fame. Hilson was a Heisman Trophy elector for many years. His broadcast style made him one of the most popular sports announcers of the time. He broadcast until his death in 1990.

Just after midnight on December 9, 1983, fire completely destroyed the building on Third Street in downtown Yankton housing the studios of WNAX. The snow and temperatures of just seven degrees hampered the efforts of the firefighters. Lost in the $1 million fire were historical memorabilia about the station, broadcasting equipment, financial records, and personal belongings. Photographs, films, tapes, and a valuable collection of over 5,000 records, some dating back to the 1920s, were destroyed.

The fire forced the station off the air at 12:03 a.m. By 5:00 a.m., it was back on the air broadcasting from the transmitter building near Mission Hill. The University of South Dakota at Springfield and radio station KQHU in Yankton lent microphones, tape machines, and other broadcasting equipment. In late December, the station moved into eight rooms in the Sheraton Hotel (now the Kelly Inn) on East Highway 50 until new facilities could be built.

WNAX began broadcasting from their new 10,000 square foot "totally integrated state of the art radio station" east of Yankton on May 20, 1985. It contained a fire alarm system, heat sensors, and a fireproof vault. The grand opening was held July 12. Roy H. Park, president of Park Communications, owner of WNAX, and South Dakota Congressman Tom Daschle cut the ribbon for the opening ceremony.

This cake was baked by Pat Halverson, niece of Marie Killian, for the grand opening of the new WNAX building in 1985.

In 1994, the insulator at the bottom of the 927-foot tower at the transmitter site was replaced with three new smaller insulators. Erhsmann Engineering Company of Yankton handled the project. The entire tower had to be lifted off its base to do the installation.

Rick Prusator became general manager of the station in February 1985. He is shown here with Marie Killian. In 1989, when WNAX was found to have the most listeners among the four radio stations operating in Yankton at the time, Prusator credited the comprehensive weather and agriculture reports, breaking news, veteran on-air personalities, country music shows, and regional sports coverage provided by the station.

In 1987, WNAX invited its listeners to the transmitter site for a picnic, reminiscent of the many held there in the 1940s and 1950s, to celebrate the station's 65th anniversary. It featured free food, entertainment, and prizes. Also attending were longtime members of the staff including, from left to right, Wynn Speece, Ed Nelson, Bob Hill, Norm Hilson, Marie Killian, and Neil Bowes.

Gene (Williams) Fiscus worked for WNAX from 1972 to 1980 and 1988 to 1995 as farm director. He was president of the National Association of Farm Broadcasters in 1979, was editor of its publication *Chats* in 1976, and won many broadcasting awards. He traveled with Secretary of Agriculture Robert Bergland to the Soviet Union and portions of Europe in 1978, one of many tours sponsored by WNAX to provide opportunities for Midwest farmers to observe farming practices in other countries.

Jon Phillips came to WNAX as market reporter in 1997 and stayed two years. He is shown with an award he received from the South Dakota Livestock Auction Market Association for his services in market reporting for listeners in the livestock business.

Brian Norton was an announcer and operations manager for the station from 1998 to 2001. He worked in both the FM and AM aspects of broadcasting.

The original Gurney Building, home of WNAX during its earlier years, stands at the corner of Second and Capital Streets. It was purchased in 2005 by the Gurney Redevelopment Group who hope to develop it into a cultural and commercial magnet for Yankton.

The first WNAX gas station still stands on Second Street in Yankton, and may be restored to compliment the new uses for the Gurney building just across the street.

The home where D. B. Gurney first set up the broadcasting equipment for WNAX is maintained in its original style and is still used as a family home. Special outlets used for broadcasting remain in several rooms.

Doug (left) and Stan Ray stand at the entrance of the WNAX transmitter building where they grew up. Their father, Bob Ray, worked as an engineer for the station at the time. The station's current engineer lives in the upstairs apartment with his family.

This workbench in the transmitter building was used by engineers to build components they needed in the years before transistors replaced tubes.

These tubes were installed in 1940. They are located in a room to one side of the more modern transmitters and are no longer used. They were made by General Electric, which, engineer Bob Ray once said, "made good toasters but not good transmitters."

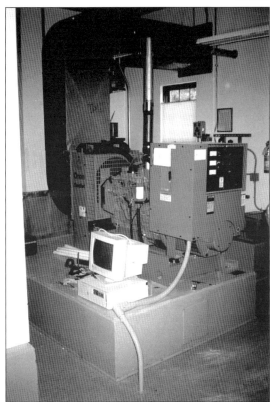

In the event of a power failure, WNAX maintains this standby generator in the transmitter building east of Yankton.

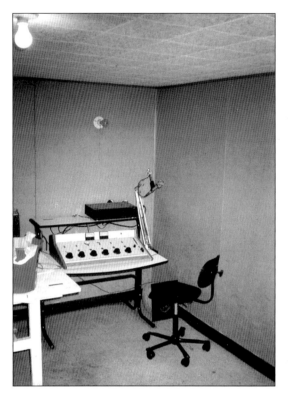

This broadcasting equipment is located in the "bomb shelter" in the basement of the transmitter building. The room has a 36 inch concrete ceiling and no openings leading to the outside except for the entrance.

The opening for the well, no longer in use, remains near the transmitter building. The well water was pumped for domestic use as well as for watering the flowers and grass in the days when the transmitter grounds were a showplace for WNAX. About six feet below the opening, a cement ledge surrounds the well pump. During World War II, the ledge was used as a bomb shelter.

In 1995, WNAX began giving away a new pickup each year in connection with a local Ford dealership. During the months of October through December, they drive the pickup to various locations to do interviews with sponsors. People register for drawings of 57 keys. Winners take their keys to the Farm Show at the Dakota Dome on the campus of the University of South Dakota. The person whose key opens the locked pickup door wins it.

Each year as a promotion, WNAX's FM station holds a contest for photographs to use in a calendar which it distributes to listeners. This photograph, submitted by Sally Kneifl of Hartington, Nebraska, won in 2005.

Terry Taylor is an advertising consultant for the Nebraska area. He started working at WNAX in 2001.

Michelle Rook (left) is the farm director and has been with the station since 1997. She will serve as president of the National Association of Farm Broadcasters in 2006. Tim Riter is the farm broadcaster.

Dee Davis is an announcer for the FM station and is the public service director. She started at WNAX in 2001. She is happy to take requests for the country songs featured on her show. She enjoys her job because she "gets paid to talk," which she likes to do anyway.

Dan Peters (left) works in the programming office and is an FM announcer. Scott Anderson is an announcer and does AM and FM continuity.

At the microphone is Steve Crawford, AM disc jockey. Standing, from left to right, are Jim Reimler, program director and AM announcer since 1989; and Steve Imming, sports director since 1992 and AM and FM announcer. Imming is the voice of the SDSU Jackrabbits for the station.

Members of the current sales department include, from left to right, Jill Sprakel and Lynette Bolle for the FM station; Larry Lanphere, sales manager east of Highway 81 in South Dakota and Minnesota; and Neil Bowes, advertising representative for western South Dakota. Bowes came to WNAX in 1961.

Business manager Lea DeJean (left) is also in charge of financial matters for the station. She has been with the station since 1994. Next is Deb Kohn, Assistant Business Manager since 1980. Standing at the right is Jackie Erickson, executive assistant, who also does the commercial logs. Seated is Michelle Nielson, receptionist, who started with WNAX in 1997.

John Cyr is the chief engineer. He came to WNAX in 2002. Only one engineer is needed at the studio now because the equipment is automated and very reliable. In the earlier years of broadcasting, transcriptions were made on huge shellac disks. Now transistors are used. Cyr is on call 24 hours a day, but, due to all the backup measures built into the system, he hardly ever receives a call when not on duty.

Judy Stratman has been with the station since 1975. She writes and produces her *Judy's Journal* program which focuses on bringing out the attributes of living and working in rural America. She highlights a different community in the area each week. Her *Sunday Morning Visit* program covers a wide range of interests and includes reports of major events and interviews with guests.

Jerry Oster, news director and information technician, came to WNAX in 1976. He is shown in front of a wall of awards he has received. Included are awards for Spot News, series/documentary, writing, newscasts, and educational coverage. In 1998, he won the Tom Brokaw award for his contributions to broadcasting in the state from the South Dakota Broadcasters Association.

Lester Tuttle has served as general manager of WNAX-AM and Big Country 104.1 FM since February 2004. He is a South Dakota native born in Winner. He received his broadcast degree and first class license from Brown Institute in Minneapolis. He has worked as a news director, sales person, sales manager, general manager, and regional manager during his more than 30 years in radio.

WNAX is currently affiliated with CBS. It is considered the premier agribusiness radio station in North America. In 2007, WNAX will celebrate its 85th anniversary. What started as a way to promote the Gurney Seed and Nursery Company has grown into a successful business devoted to meeting the needs of its listeners across the area it covers. It lives up to its current motto—"Your Five State Neighbor."

# ACROSS AMERICA, PEOPLE ARE DISCOVERING SOMETHING WONDERFUL. *THEIR HERITAGE.*

Arcadia Publishing is the leading local history publisher in the United States. With more than 3,000 titles in print and hundreds of new titles released every year, Arcadia has extensive specialized experience chronicling the history of communities and celebrating America's hidden stories, bringing to life the people, places, and events from the past. To discover the history of other communities across the nation, please visit:

# www.arcadiapublishing.com

Customized search tools allow you to find regional history books about the town where you grew up, the cities where your friends and family live, the town where your parents met, or even that retirement spot you've been dreaming about.